PICTORIAL
GREAT STUFF
MUSEUMS OF NOVA SCOTIA

Historic sites, people, artifacts and much more

James-StoneHouse Publications
Limited
PO Box 428
Dartmouth, Nova Scotia
Canada B2Y 3Y5

Canadian Cataloguing in
Publication Data
Great Stuff
Museums of Nova Scotia

ISBN 0-921128-39-8

1. Museums — Nova Scotia —
Pictorial works

AM21.N6G73 1993   069'.09716'0222
C92-098738-9

Printed for James-StoneHouse
Publications Ltd. in Hong Kong

Graphic Design: William Richardson
Text and Editing: Paddy Muir
Typesetting: Karen Kavanaugh
Production: Lisa Whitman, Peter Shortt
General Manager: J. Daniel Sargeant
Photo Credits: See page 104
On behalf of the Museum
Awareness Committee: Joan
Waldron, Jim Tupper

As the 21st-century looms, time seems to rush past faster and faster. The world around us changes at an ever-accelerating rate. Yet, as we hurtle into the future, our past becomes increasingly important. The past offers us a benchmark, a point from which to measure the present. It provides a connection with bygone generations, a connection so easily lost in a world of mobility, rapid techological change and disappearing traditions. The past offers us both roots and invaluable perspective.

Nova Scotia, Nouvelle Ecosse, New Scotland - nowhere in Canada do the roots go deeper or are more treasured than here. And nowhere is it easier to discover them today. Dotted throughout the province, dozens of museums have carefully collected and preserved our past - from sharp stone tools fashioned centuries ago by the Mi'kmaq, to a steam mill, revolutionary in its day. Each museum holds pieces of the puzzle - a day-by-day diary of an early Loyalist settler, a merchant's accounts, a fire engine, a china collection, a portrait. Housed in a fisherman's cottage, a farmhouse or magnificent homes built for wealthy families, museums open doors into the lives of the humble and the aristocratic.

For people interested in genealogy, the archives in many of the province's treasure houses preserve priceless family histories. Museums also offer a window on the history of the land itself - its geology, its plants and its animals - from the time of the dinosaurs to the present day.

Museums not only educate but also entertain. Some ancestors turn out to have been rum-runners, salmon-poachers and privateers; collectors of the bizarre as well as the beautiful, adherents of strange and wonderful lives. They were craftspeople and farmers, miners and fishermen, naturalists, industrialists and inventors. Many came from distant places to a hard and sometimes forbidding land. Often against the odds, they made it their home.

Across Nova Scotia clusters of committed people have rescued the past, sometimes from the brink, and provided safekeeping for future generations. Many are volunteer members of local historical societies, others are skilled staff of community museums and various branches of the Nova Scotia Museum Complex. This book is a tribute to their vigilance and enthusiasm, and a visual celebration of just a few aspects of our province's rich natural and human history.

When the world of today seems unfathomable, distressing or just plain too fast, escape into the past. Nova Scotia's community museums, branches of the Nova Scotia Museum Complex and federal historic sites will make you most welcome. We promise you'll discover a host of fascinating places filled with no end of great stuff!

South Shore

Annapolis Valley

Halifax-Dartmouth

Eastern Region

Cape Breton

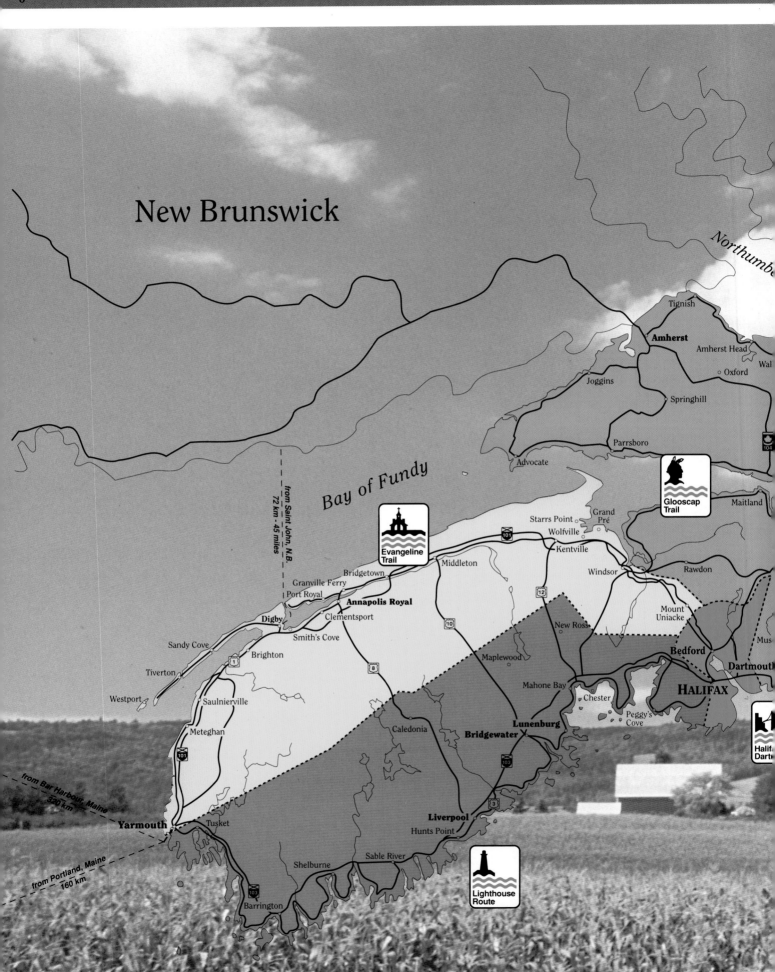

New Brunswick

Northumbe

Tignish

Amherst

Amherst Head

Wal

Oxford

Joggins

Springhill

Parrsboro

Advocate

Maitland

Glooscap Trail

Bay of Fundy

from Saint John, N.B.
72 km - 45 miles

Starrs Point

Grand Pré

Wolfville

Kentville

Evangeline Trail

101

12

Windsor

Rawdon

Middleton

Bridgetown

Granville Ferry

Port Royal

Annapolis Royal

Clementsport

10

Mount Uniacke

New Ross

Digby

Smith's Cove

Bedford

Mus

Sandy Cove

Brighton

8

Maplewood

Dartmouth

Tiverton

Mahone Bay

Chester

HALIFAX

Westport

Saulnierville

Peggy's Cove

Halif
Dart

Meteghan

Caledonia

Lunenburg

Bridgewater

101

from Bar Harbour, Maine
350 km

103

Liverpool

Hunts Point

3

Yarmouth

Tusket

from Portland, Maine
160 km

Shelburne

Sable River

Lighthouse Route

Barrington

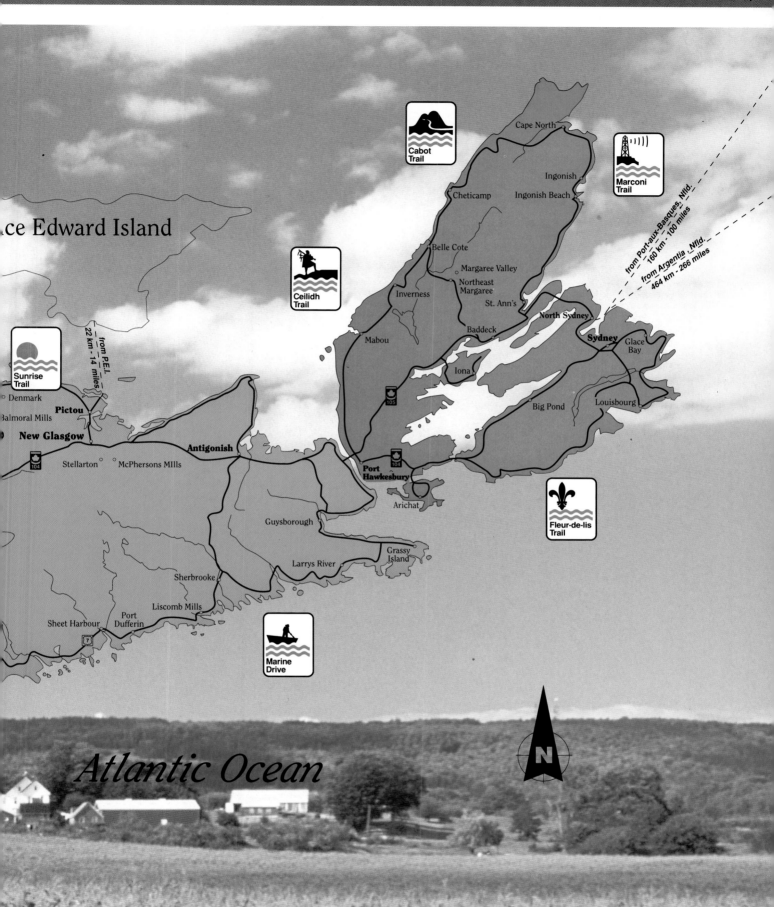

Prince Edward Island

Cabot Trail

Marconi Trail

Ceilidh Trail

Cape North

Ingonish

Cheticamp
Ingonish Beach

Belle Cote

Margaree Valley

Northeast Margaree

Inverness

St. Ann's

North Sydney

Baddeck

Sydney
Glace Bay

Mabou

Iona

Big Pond
Louisbourg

from Port-aux-Basques, Nfld.
160 km - 100 miles

from Argentia, Nfld.
464 km - 266 miles

Sunrise Trail

from P.E.I.
22 km - 14 miles

Denmark

Pictou

Balmoral Mills

New Glasgow

Antigonish

Stellarton   McPhersons MIlls

Port Hawkesbury

Arichat

Fleur-de-lis Trail

Guysborough

Grassy Island

Larrys River

Sherbrooke

Liscomb Mills

Sheet Harbour   Port Dufferin

Marine Drive

Atlantic Ocean

N

Mill on the River
John Elliott Woolford (1778-1866)
Painting shows Shelburne Harbour and town, 1817
Collection of the Nova Scotia Museum

Tusket

THE OLDEST STANDING
COURTHOUSE & GAOL
IN
CANADA
1805 - 1976
ARGYLE TOWNSHIP

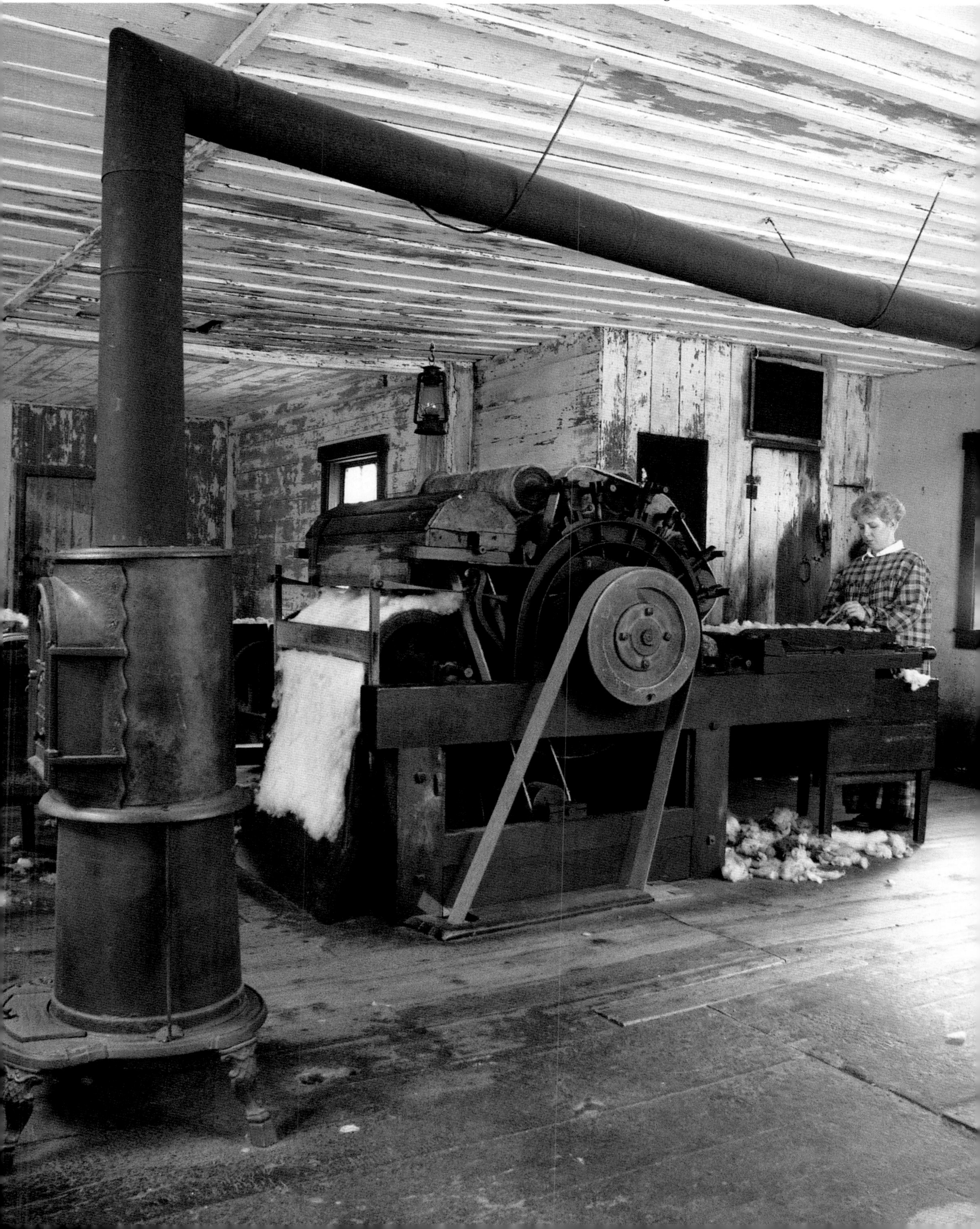

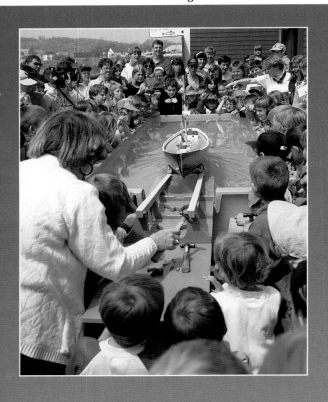

Acadians repairing a dyke, circa 1720, at Belleisle, N.S.
Azor Vienneau (1936-   )
Latex on masonite
Collection of the Nova Scotia Museum

Mount Uniacke

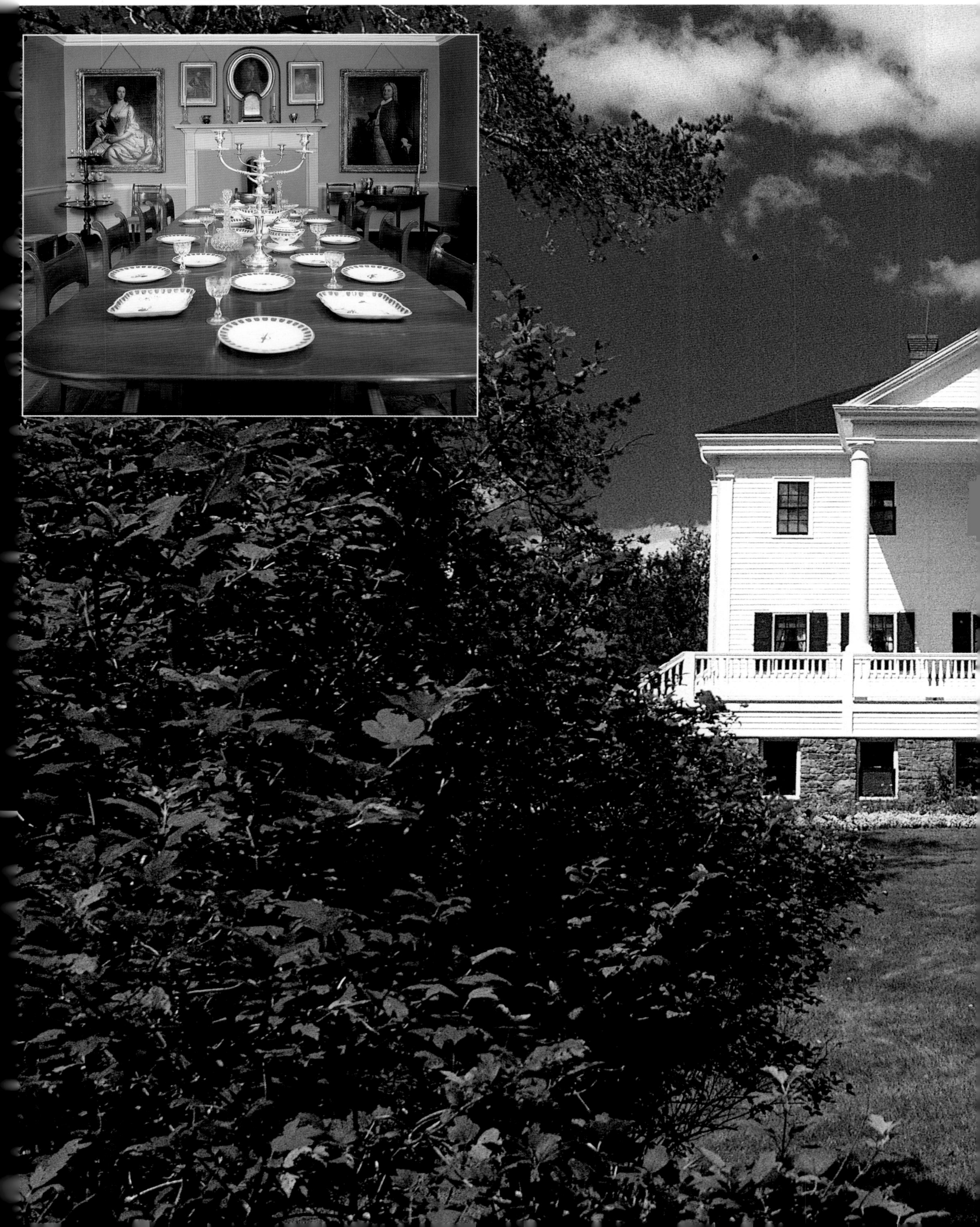

Halifax from Windmill Pier, Dartmouth
Robert Wilkie (1828-1903)
Oil on canvas, circa 1852
Collection of the Art Gallery of Nova Scotia

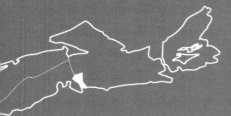

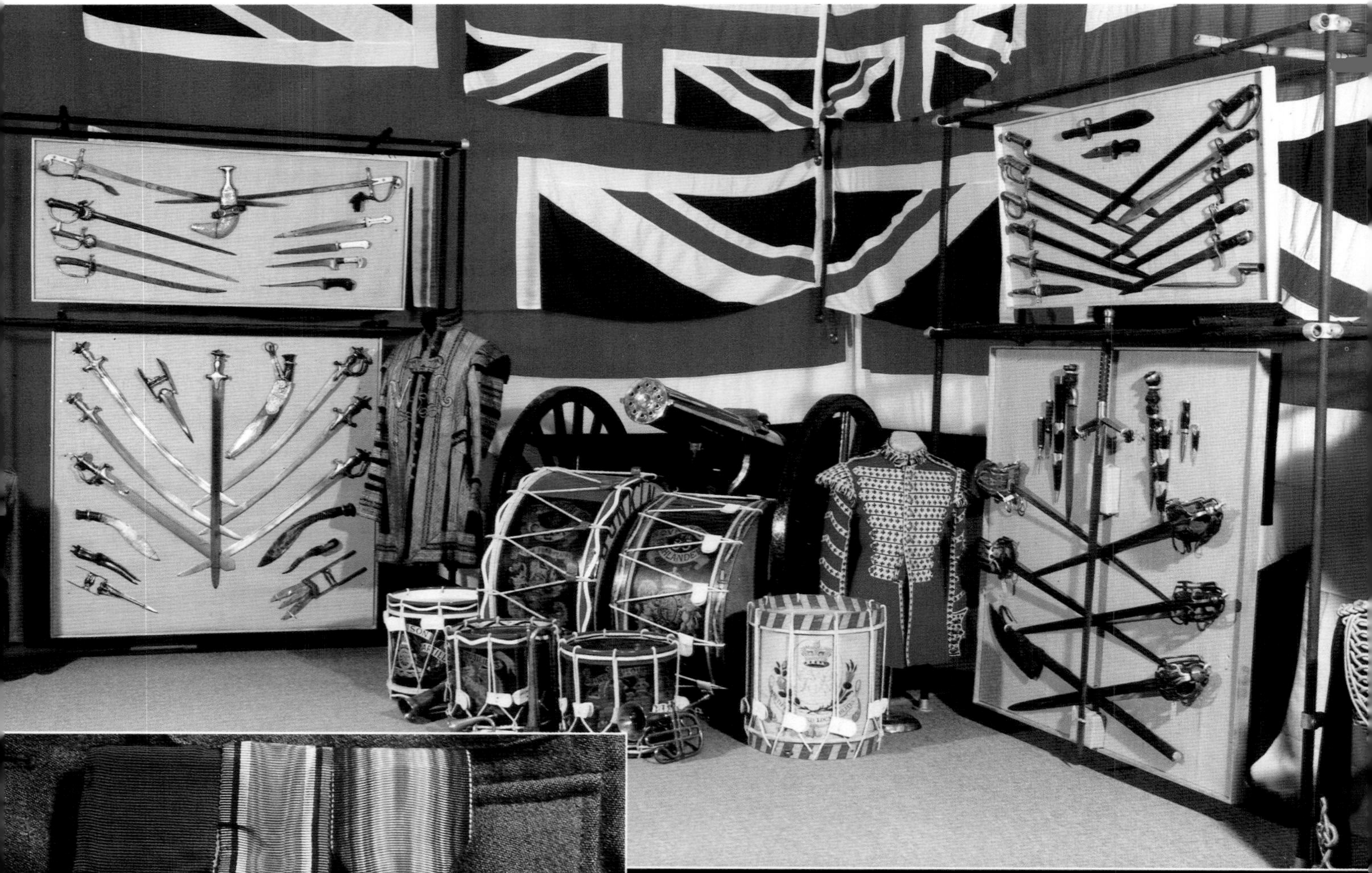

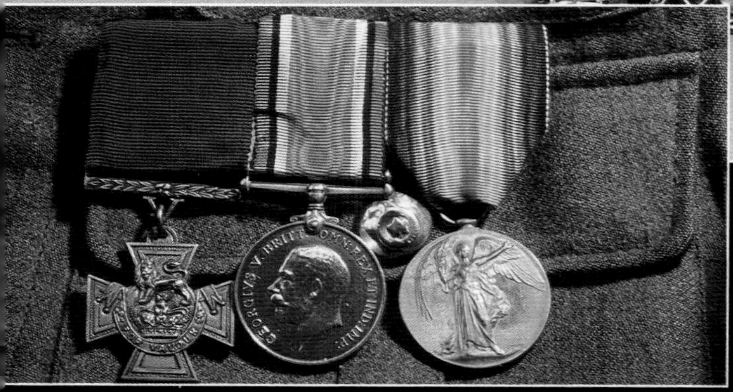

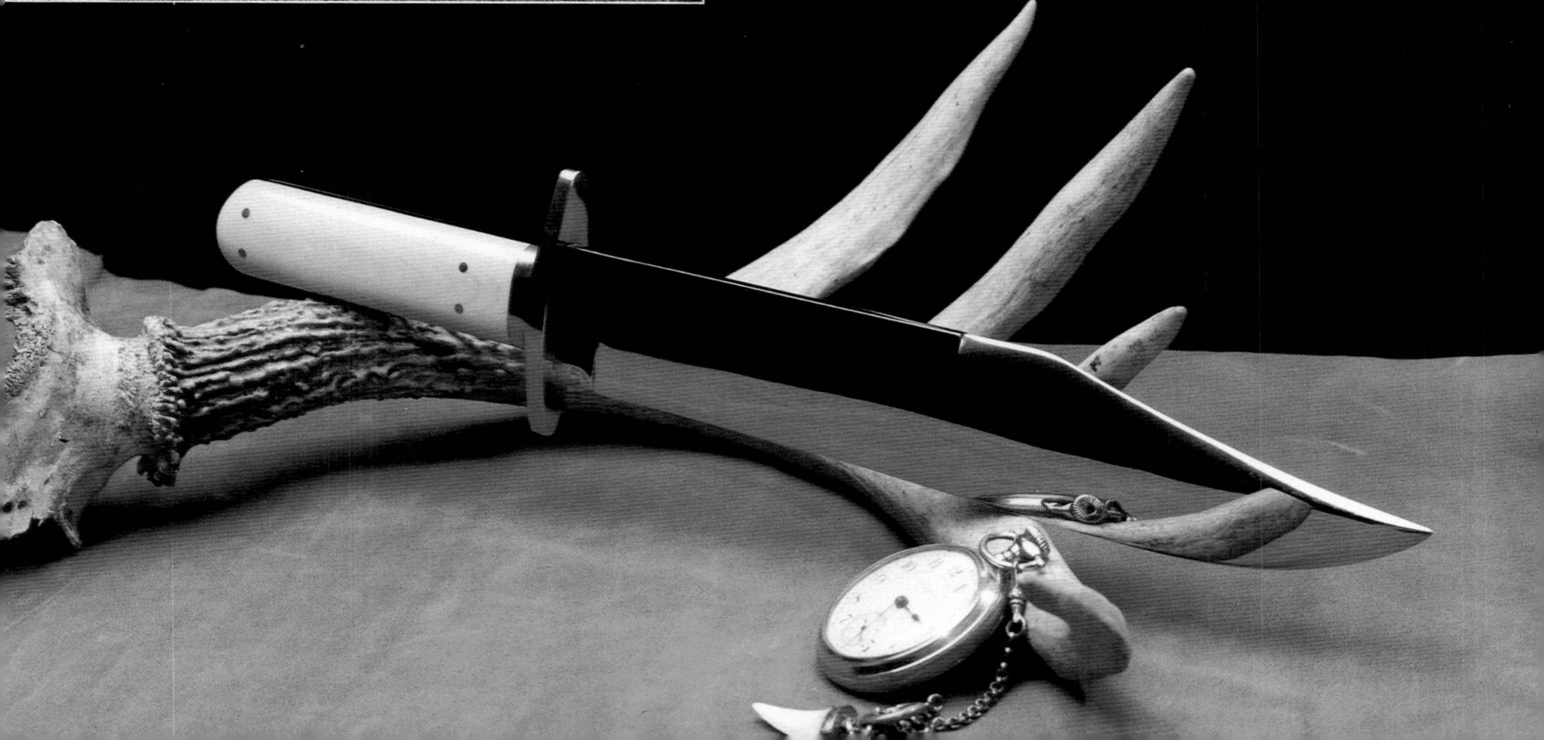

Digging Oysters, Northumberland Straits
William G.R. Hind (1833-1889)
Watercolour with ink, circa 1875
Collection of the Public Archives of Nova Scotia

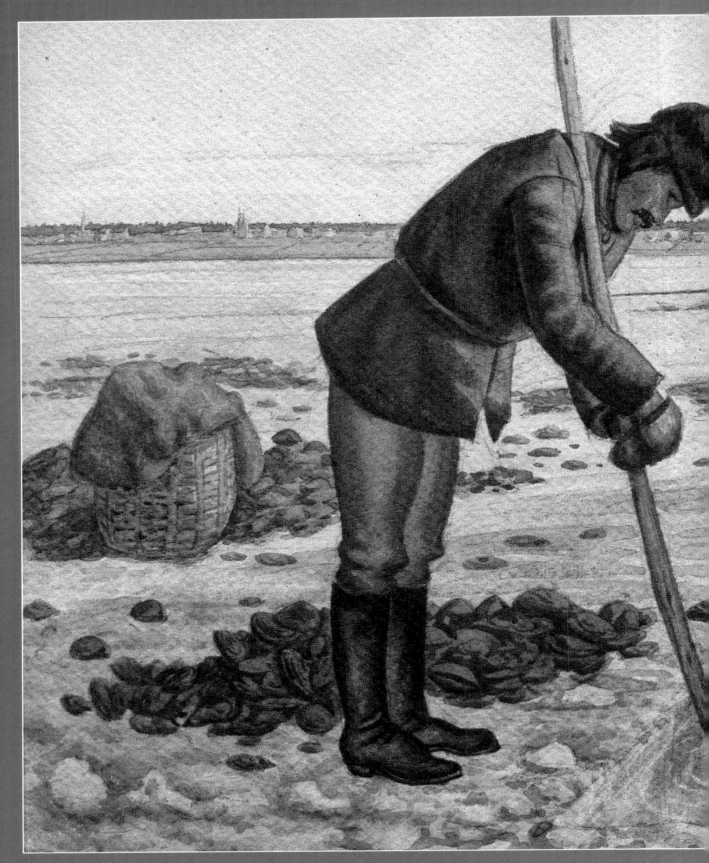

Maitland

Antigonish

Island of Cape Breton (Nova Scotia): The Margaree Valley (Blue-berrying)
William G.R. Hind (1833-1889)
Oil on paper, circa 1872
Collection of the Public Archives of Nova Scotia

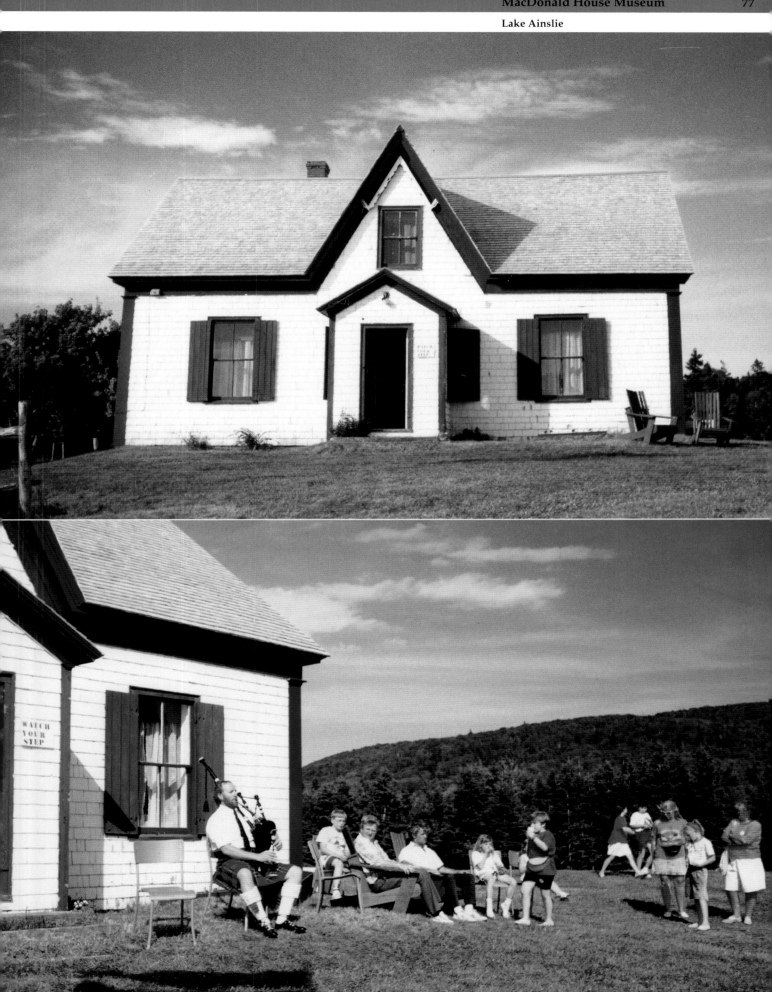

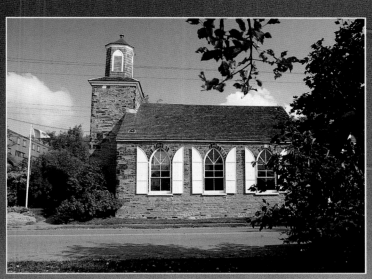

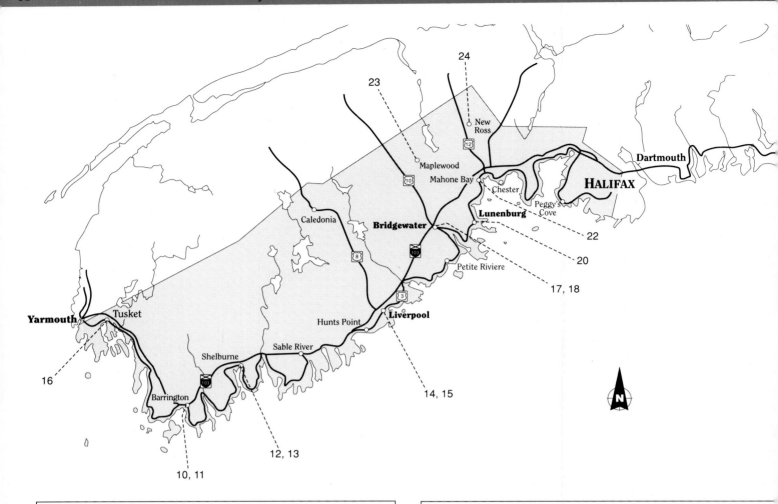

Argyle Township Courthouse and Gaol   p.16

P.O. Box 101
Tusket, Nova Scotia B0W 3M0
(902) 648-2493

Built in the picturesque Loyalist village of Tusket, between 1801 and 1805, the Argyle Township Courthouse and Gaol is Canada's oldest standing courthouse. The courtroom, grand jury room and judge's chamber, with period furnishings, occupy the second floor, while the old gaol (jail) cells and the gaol-keeper's room are found on the ground floor. The dungeon-like gaol provides a startling look at the conditions under which prisoners lived in the 19th century. In contrast, the courtroom is a room of spartan elegance. The judge's podium offers views of the beautiful Tusket River through almost all of the room's seven 12-over-12-paned windows. At the rear of the first floor, the archives contain many documents dating back to the 1700s. There is also an extensive local history and genealogical collection, and the largest microfilm collection in southwestern Nova Scotia. Guided tours of the building are available throughout the day, June to September. Other times by appointment. Archives open year-round.

Barrington Meetinghouse/
Barrington Woolen Mill   p.11

Route 3
Barrington, Nova Scotia
(902) 637-2185

Built in 1765 for the 50 Cape Cod families who founded Barrington Township, the **Barrington Meetinghouse** is the oldest non-conformist house of worship still existing in Canada. It was in use for almost 100 years and rescued for posterity in 1889. In 1979 it was turned over to the Province of Nova Scotia. The adjacent graveyard, where many of the early townspeople are buried, is of particular interest. The two-and-a-half storey, water-turbine-powered **Barrington Woolen Mill** was typical of many small manufacturing operations established during the latter part of the 19th century. It was based on a local resource and served a local market. Over the years the fortunes of the mill ebbed and flowed with the economy but it operated until 1962 when the building with its unique collection of carding machines, spinning jennies, looms and wool-scouring equipment became part of the Nova Scotia Museum Complex. Both museums are managed by the Cape Sable Historical Society. Open June 15-September 30.

DesBrisay Museum   p.18
Jubilee Road, Box 353
Bridgewater, Nova Scotia B4V 2W9
(902) 543-4033

Nestled in the Bridgewater Woodland Gardens, the DesBrisay Museum boasts one of the oldest collections in the Atlantic region. Through modern, designed exhibits, visitors can discover the Town and the County's natural, industrial and cultural heritage and learn about the Museum's own history. Video presentations, gallery quizzes, interactive displays and a year-round special events program ensure appeal to visitors of every age. The decorative arts are represented by works of two Nova Scotia women artists: Christiana Morris, the 19th-century Micmac who created birchbark panels with traditional porcupine quill decoration for DesBrisay's famed hooded cradle, and Alice Hagen, Nova Scotia's pioneer artist potter who taught and created in nearby Mahone Bay. A second gallery hosts temporary exhibitions of collections from local, national and international sources through the National Exhibition Centre Program. Professional interpreters are available to assist visitors and the Friends of the DesBrisay Museum operate a well-stocked gift shop. Open year-round, hours vary by season.

The Dory Shop   p.12
Dock Street
Shelburne, Nova Scotia
(902) 875-3219

For almost 100 years the dory was one of the most important small boats in the Atlantic provinces and parts of New England. Usually built with a bottom length of 12-16 feet, a dory could carry two people equipped with bait and fishing gear for handlining or trawl fishing. They were an integral part of the offshore fishery, especially on the Grand Banks of Newfoundland. When the John Williams Dory Shop was established in 1880, it was part of a dory-building industry which, at one time, included at least seven shops along the Shelburne waterfront. During the early part of the century the Williams Shop employed five to seven men and produced 350 dories per year, most of which were sold to Nova Scotian and American fishing captains. Visitors to the Dory Shop can see from start to finish how dories were built. Managed by the Shelburne Historical Society for the Nova Scotia Museum Complex. Open daily July 1-August 31.

Fisheries Museum of the Atlantic   p.20
Bluenose Drive, P.O. Box 1363
Lunenburg, Nova Scotia B0J 2C0
(902) 634-4794

The Fisheries Museum of the Atlantic consists of buildings and vessels on the waterfront in Lunenburg's 'Old Town' section, the largest designated historic district in Canada. It celebrates the east coast fishing heritage with exhibits, an aquarium, activities and authentic fishing vessels. Demonstrations include small boat building, fish filleting, lobster trap making, mat hooking, canvas work, knitting and quilting. Exhibits are located in the buildings and aboard the Museum vessels *Theresa E. Connor,* the last schooner to fish from Lunenburg, and *Cape Sable,* a steel-hulled trawler. Visitors can board the vessels and talk with fishermen about the days 'on the Banks'. Exhibits include three floors of displays, vessel models, inshore boats, a *Bluenose* exhibit and an audio-visual theatre. The site also includes a gift shop, a restaurant and plenty of free parking. Plan to visit the Fisheries Museum of the Atlantic - there's something to interest everyone. Part of the Nova Scotia Museum Complex. Open daily June 1 - Oct 15.

Parkdale-Maplewood Community Museum   p.23
3005 Barss Corner Road
Maplewood, Lunenburg County
R.R. # 1 Barss Corner, Nova Scotia B0R 1A0
(902) 644-2893

A leisurely 45-minute drive inland from Blockhouse takes the traveller up the scenic Cornwall Road to Maplewood. Located on the Community Fair Grounds, this country museum occupies a former lodge hall and the attached new (1984) exhibit hall. Folk arts and crafts are the focus of the collection with baskets, wood carvings, quilts, knitting, rugs, handmade tools and furniture on display. These treasures, plus Victorian collectibles, local history items, photos, books, family and community histories, make this collection a favourite of museum buffs. The Museum grounds feature a developing heritage vegetable garden, antique roses, medicinal herbs, traditional perennials; native plants, herbs and shrubs, plus a picnic area. Craft demonstrations and musical entertainment at the Maple Syrup Festival (April), Community Fair (August) and Heritage Blueberry Festival (September). Open daily, June-Labour Day, or by appointment.

Perkins House   p.14
105 Main Street, P.O. Box 1078
Liverpool, Nova Scotia B0T 1K0
(902) 354-4058

"Extream Cold, very windy & the Snow Flies, & makes it the most Tedious day we have had this winter, and The Frost the hardest. my Ink has been froze the most of the day on the Table near the Fire." So wrote Connecticut native Simeon Perkins in January 1780 in the meticulous diary he kept for almost 50 years. Perkins became one of Liverpool's leading citizens, a merchant and ship-owner, a Colonel of the local militia, Judge and Member of the Legislative Assembly. The simple Connecticut house he had built in 1766 and extended twice over the years to accommodate his growing family, entertained governors, privateer captains and itinerant preachers in its day. Today, complete with a copy of the famous diary and furnished to the period, it is operated by the Queens County Historical Society for the Nova Scotia Museum Complex. Open to the public June 1 to October 15.

Queens County Museum   p.15
109 Main Street, P.O. Box 1078
Liverpool, Nova Scotia B0T 1K0
(902) 354-4058

Liverpool - the Micmac called it Ogomkegea, the French called it Le Port du Rossignol. In the mid-1700s the New Englanders named it Liverpool when they created this picturesque little town nestled at the mouth of the Mersey River. The sounds of shipbuilding and sailors readying their vessels for travel and trade were not uncommon in this early community. In times of war the Liverpool privateers protected their own shores and captured ships flying the flags of enemy countries. Some of their cannons are still to be seen in and around our town. Two of them are displayed on the grounds of the Queens County Museum. Inside the building our heritage is illustrated by exhibits featuring the Micmac, Early Settlement, Privateering, Forestry, Shipbuilding and other subjects that emphasize our historic past. Queens County Museum - a place to remember. Open year-round, hours vary by season.

Ross Farm Museum   p.24
Route 12
New Ross, Nova Scotia B0J 2M0
(902) 689-2210

Once the home of five generations of the Ross family, this 56-acre farm was first cleared from the forest by Captain William Ross in 1816. Today at this living museum of agriculture you can see traditional breeds of animals and crops, ride a horse-drawn wagon and watch a blacksmith at work. Taste and smell good food being prepared in the restored 19th-century Rosebank Cottage. See wooden staves being cut in the stave mill, then chat with the cooper as he makes them into barrels. You can also examine a collection of farm implements and artifacts that trace the development of agriculture from its Nova Scotian and North American beginnings in 1603, through to 1917. The Pedlar's Shop offers produce from the farm kitchen and articles made on the farm and in the community for sale. Operated by the New Ross District Museum Society for the Nova Scotia Museum Complex. Open seasonally.

Ross-Thomson House   p.13
Charlotte Lane
Shelburne, Nova Scotia
(902) 875-3219

By 1784, Loyalists on the run from the American Revolution had swelled Shelburne's small population to 10,000. With this wave of settlement there were many opportunists who saw their chance in commercial endeavours. These included George and Robert Ross, sons of a Scottish merchant, who traded Shelburne's pine boards, cod and pickled herring in foreign ports for salt, tobacco, molasses and dry goods which they sold to the new settlers. In operation until the 1880s, the Ross-Thomson house is the only original store building remaining in Shelburne. Constructed of wood on a granite foundation, with heavy planked doors and birch-bark trimmed windows, the building shows the influence of New England architecture in the 18th-century tradition. It is restored to 1820s condition and operated as part of the Shelburne Historic Block by the Shelburne Historical Society for the Nova Scotia Museum Complex. Open June 1-Oct 15.

Seal Island Light and Cape Sable Historical Society   p.10

Route 3
Barrington, Nova Scotia
(902) 637-2185

The Cape Sable Historical Society is a community museum which offers the visitor a chance to look at the record of Barrington Township through artifacts, archives, photos, tape recordings and publications. The Seal Island Light is a reconstruction which houses the original Seal Island lighthouse lantern and operating mechanism first used in 1831. Visitors can climb to the top of the lighthouse, enjoy the magnificent view and see artifacts relating to the sea, navigation, whaling and shipwrecks. The other prize possession of the Cape Sable Historical Society is a handwoven mural by the late Bessie Murray. It features a woven highlander wearing the first example of the Nova Scotia tartan. This is on display at the nearby Barrington Woolen Mill. Open June 15-September 30.

Settlers' Museum and Cultural Centre   p.22

578 Main Street, P.O. Box 583
Mahone Bay, Nova Scotia B0K 2E0
(902) 624-6263

The Settlers' Museum is housed in the Benjamin Begin House (circa 1850) with its distinctive 'Lunenburg bump' - a two-storey front porch indigenous to Lunenburg County. Furnished to period, the parlour features a painted ceiling and a faux marble fireplace. The kitchen is typical with large fireplace, bake oven, and furnishings made locally. Benjamin Begin was a sailmaker and the Wooden Boat building exhibit, including models, tools and details on local shipyards, is housed in his sail loft. Interpretive displays on the 1754 settling of the area by foreign Protestants and early local architecture help visitors identify Heritage houses in the area. A ceramics gallery contains a selection of items from the Inglis/Quinlan Collection gathered from 1895 to 1950, including typical local household tableware of the late 18th and early 19th century: creamware, lustreware, transfer-printed earthenware, ironstone and porcelain. Other exhibits include toys and early photographs of the town. Hours vary by season.

Wile Carding Mill   p.17

Pearl Street and Victoria Road
Route 325
Bridgewater, Nova Scotia
(902) 543-4033

Built in 1860 and in continuous operation for more than a century, Dean Wile's water-powered carding mill is the last of seven early small industries located along Pleasant River in what was then the industrial centre of Bridgewater. When the carding mill was built, there were 16,786 sheep in Lunenburg County, about 5% of the sheep population in the province. Farmers from the county and beyond arrived by ox cart, wagon or even boat to have their wool carded and batted before taking it home for spinning, weaving and quilt-making. At the height of the sheepshearing season, the mill operated 24 hours a day, six days a week and employed five people, mostly women, to keep up with demand. The mill building and the seven-horsepower waterwheel have been restored and the picking, carding and batting machines on display are the originals. Today the Mill is managed by the DesBrisay Museum for the Nova Scotia Museum Complex. Open daily June 1-October 15.

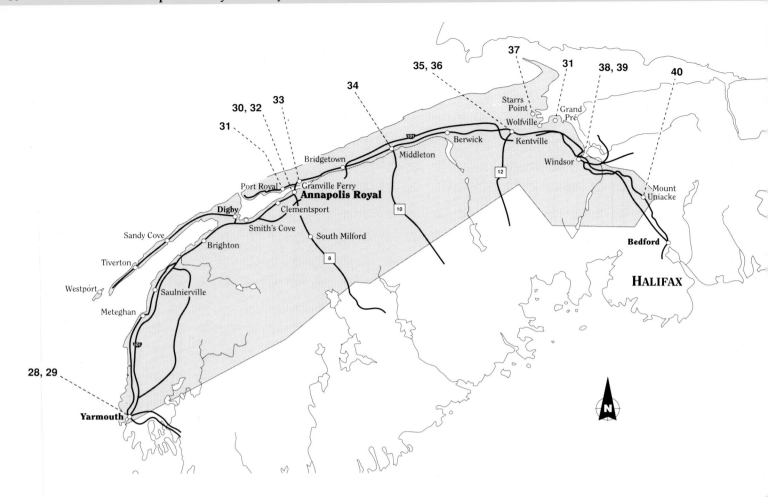

Annapolis Royal Historic Gardens   p.30

441 St. George Street, P.O. Box 278
Annapolis Royal, Nova Scotia B0S 1A0
(902) 532-7018

Stroll through ten acres of gardens and displays
illustrating the history of gardening and horticulture
in Nova Scotia. Highlights include a Victorian
Garden, the Governor's Garden, an Acadian Garden
and the rose collection. Seven acres of dyked
marshlands and a fifty-acre Ducks Unlimited
sanctuary complement the Gardens. Open May
through October.

Annapolis Valley Macdonald Museum   p.34

21 School Street, P.O. Box 925
Middleton, Nova Scotia B0S 1P0
(902) 825-6116

Nestled in the heart of the Annapolis Valley,
Canada's first consolidated school - the Macdonald
School - has sat among the maples on a lovely
landscaped lot since 1903. It is now the home of the
Annapolis Valley Macdonald Museum. The museum
offers the visitor a trip back in time exploring the
local artifacts of the "Rusty Nail" collection, a
recreated general store from the Depression era, and
a circa-1940 classroom filled with memorabilia of
bygone school days. The large collection of antique
clocks and watches is a major attraction. The Valley
Art Gallery displays the talents of local artists and
craftspeople - always something new and different.
For the genealogy enthusiast there is a spacious,
well-equipped research library with a vast amount of
information on Annapolis County families. Located
in an attached greenhouse, an extensive exhibit will
guide the visitor through the natural history of the
Annapolis Valley region. Open year-round, hours
vary by season.

Blair House Museum   p.36
Kentville Agricultural Centre
Kentville, Nova Scotia B4N 1J5
(902) 678-1093

The Blair House Museum, located on the Kentville Agricultural Centre grounds in the heart of Nova Scotia's beautiful Annapolis Valley, offers both an interesting and an educational look at the history of the apple industry in the province, as well as at the modern research being done at the Centre. The Nova Scotia Fruit Growers' Association wing tells the history of the apple industry in Nova Scotia through pictures, stories and artifacts. Barrel-making tools, apple baskets, peelers, even an old sprayer, show how things were done over half a century ago. The Agriculture Canada wing offers a look at both the past and present research performed at the Centre. All display rooms complement each other to give visitors a well-rounded look at the industry - past and present. Open weekdays, May to September. Rhododendron Sunday, the second Sunday in June is a visual extravaganza not to be missed.

Firefighters' Museum of Nova Scotia   p.29
451 Main Street
Yarmouth, Nova Scotia B5A 1G9
(902) 742-5525

Follow the history of firefighting in Nova Scotia since the early 1800s in Canada's only provincial Firefighters' Museum. The rare collection of equipment, machines and memorabilia includes fire buckets, hand-drawn pumpers and Canada's oldest horse-drawn fire engine. It also contains many smaller items, such as hose reels, helmets, shoulder flashes, badges and pictures of many famous fires. There is a library on site and a gift shop with fire-fighting-related articles for sale. A National Exhibition Centre at the Museum regularly features national and provincial travelling exhibits and collections. The Firefighters' Museum is part of the Nova Scotia Museum Complex. Open year-round, hours vary by season.

Haliburton House   p.38
Clifton Avenue
Windsor, Nova Scotia
(902) 424-6478

Born in Windsor in 1796, Thomas Chandler Haliburton was a lawyer, judge, historian and member of both the Nova Scotia Legislative Assembly and the British House of Commons. He was also the first Canadian author to gain international recognition, as the creator of Sam Slick the Yankee clock peddler whose witty sayings are still commonly used. Haliburton's one-and-a-half-storey wooden villa set on a 40-acre estate overlooking Windsor was built in 1836. The gardens were created by Mrs. Haliburton and admired by all who visited. The house has undergone many changes since Haliburton's day. It was acquired as a historic site by the Province in 1939 and furnished with items of local interest. Some of the objects were owned by Haliburton himself, including his desk and some furniture. Also on display is part of the Weldon Collection of china assembled by Haliburton's daughter. Part of the Nova Scotia Museum Complex. Open June 1-October 15

National Historic Sites of Western Nova Scotia   p.31
Canadian Parks Service
Historic Properties, Upper Water Street
Halifax, Nova Scotia B3J 1S9
(902) 426-3436

Canada is world renowned for its national parks and historic sites - and for good reason. Our parks and sites offer an opportunity to discover Canada's unique natural and cultural heritage. Nowhere is this diversity more evident than at the National Historic Sites of Fort Anne, Port Royal, Grand Pré and Fort Edward. Visit Fort Anne and explore the officers' quarters and powder magazine. Walk the ramparts and re-live the struggle between France and England for control of North America. Port Royal's costumed interpreters will bring one of North America's earliest European settlements to life. While enjoying the beautiful gardens at Grand Pré, learn about the Acadian culture and deportation of 1755. At Fort Edward, discover the oldest surviving blockhouse in Canada. At each site, friendly and knowledgeable staff will help you make the most of your visit with special tours and presentations. Watch for the Beaver Symbol on highway signs. It will lead you to vacation experiences of a lifetime.

North Hills Museum   p.33
Off Route 1
Granville Ferry, Nova Scotia
(902) 532-7754

A magnificent collection of 18th-century furnishings can be found in this small wood-framed house overlooking the Annapolis Basin. Robert Patterson, a retired banker and antique collector, bequeathed the house and furnishings to the Province of Nova Scotia in 1974. Visitors will see many fine examples of oak, walnut and mahogany furniture; 18th- and 19th-century English porcelain and 18th-century glass and paintings. Among the paintings are works by John Hoppner, George Chinnery, Sir Francis Chantrey, Francis Cotes and George Morland. The house was known as Rumsey Farm until the early 1800s, then later it was called the Amberman House. Robert Patterson renamed the house North Hills when he purchased it in 1964. North Hills is operated by the Historic Restoration Society of Annapolis County for the Nova Scotia Museum Complex. Open June 1 to October 15.

O'Dell House/Robertson House   p.32
Lower St. George Street, P.O. Box 503
Annapolis Royal, Nova Scotia B0S 1A0
(902) 532-7754 or 532-2041 (summer only)

The Historic Restoration Society operates two museums located in the once-bustling waterfront district of Annapolis Royal. The **O'Dell House**, built in 1869, was an inn and tavern catering to the travelling public. Some of the rooms are furnished as they would have been in the 1870s, while others house rotating displays on shipbuilding and shipping in the Annapolis area, Victorian attitudes towards death, and items from the extensive collection of 18th- to 20th-century costumes, one of the largest in the Maritimes. The **Robertson House** (circa 1784) contains a display of working printing presses and the Museum of Childhood - dolls and accessories, toys and games, books and costumes, and items from local schoolrooms covering nearly 200 years. Of special interest are the chairs, shoes and dresses of the "Fairy Sisters", Cassie and Victoria Foster, two famous 19th-century midgets born in the area. Open daily June 1 to September 30.

The Old Kings Courthouse Museum   p.35
37 Cornwallis Street
Kentville, Nova Scotia B4N 2E2
(902) 678-6237

The Old Kings Courthouse Museum is located in Kentville, the 'shiretown' of Kings County. The turn-of-the-century brick Courthouse was the seat of justice in Kings County from 1903 until 1980. Visitors to the Museum will find exhibits which relate the cultural and natural history of the County. Permanent exhibits include: a bird collection from Canadian ornithologist, Dr. Robie Tufts; a rock and fossil collection; a Canadian Parks Service exhibit on the New England Planters; a Victorian parlour; and the Courtroom where the woodwork has been hand-grained to simulate oak. If you look closely you will find animals sketched into the grain of the wood. An important site for researchers, the Museum houses a library and community histories archives. The Genealogical Committee of the Kings Historical Society is located in the basement. Here you'll find family genealogies, Kings County cemetery records and New England Planter genealogical material. Open year-round on weekdays, hours vary by season.

Prescott House   p.37
Starr's Point, off Route 358
Near Wolfville, Nova Scotia
(902) 424-6478

Charles Ramage Prescott made his fortune as a Halifax merchant, but earned his lasting reputation as a horticulturalist who introduced and developed varieties of apples and other plants particularly suitable to Nova Scotia. He built his fine Georgian-style home of local brick, from 1814-1816 and called it Acacia Grove because of the numerous acacia trees planted on the property. After Charles Prescott's death in 1859, the estate gradually fell into neglect until the 1930s when it was bought, restored and refurnished by his great-granddaughter, Miss Mary Allison Prescott, with some of the items that had belonged to the Prescott family. She lived in the house herself with her two sisters from 1942 until her death in 1969. The estate and its attractive garden overlooks the agriculturally rich, dyked lands of the Cornwallis River. Part of the Nova Scotia Museum Complex, Prescott House has been designated a National and a Provincial Historic Site. Open June 1 - October 15.

Shand House   p.39
Avon Street
Windsor, Nova Scotia
(902) 424-6478

When the Shand family built this ornate late-Victorian house in 1890-91 it was the latest thing, equipped with central heating, closets, electric lighting and even indoor plumbing. Finished with handmade panelling in cherry and oak the major rooms contain many other fittings typical of the period. Today the house remains furnished as it was when the Shands lived there, reflecting the style of the period when it was furnished and decorated. As well as imported items, the furniture includes several fine examples of items mass-made at a local factory which operated until 1928. Such furniture was a novelty at that time. Few changes were made over the years and most of the things acquired and used by the Shand family from 1891 to 1920 are still there, including memorabilia from Clifford Shand's days as a high-wheeled bicycle racer. Following the death of the Shand's daughter, Gwendolyn, the house became a branch of the Nova Scotia Museum Complex. Open June 1-October 15.

Uniacke House   p.40
Route 1
Mount Uniacke, Nova Scotia

When Attorney-General Richard John Uniacke built his grand summer home from 1813 -15, he ordered mahogany furniture custom crafted by George Adams of London. This fine furniture, some of it with the maker's labels still attached, remains in the house along with other original furnishings, such as John Uniacke's books, his armchair and desk, and other items added during a family occupancy that lasted until 1949 when the house and contents were acquired by the Province of Nova Scotia. Of note among the later additions are portraits by Robert Feke and John Singleton Copley. From the great fourposter beds, dressers and washstands of the upstairs bedrooms to the huge fireplace and cook's quarters of the basement kitchen, Uniacke House offers visitors a vivid glimpse of 19th-century life among Nova Scotia's gentry. The survival of this house, one of Canada's finest examples of the Neo-Classical style in colonial architecture, with its contents is very rare. Part of the Nova Scotia Museum Complex. Open June 1 - October 15.

Yarmouth County Museum   p.28
22 Collins Street
Yarmouth, Nova Scotia B5A 3C8
(902) 742-5539

"One of the finest community museums in North America" and "a 'real gem' " were two of the phrases used to describe the Yarmouth County Museum in 1990 when it won a prestigious Canadian Parks Service Heritage Award. The Museum maintains a large and significant collection of artifacts, primarily from the Victorian era and with a special emphasis on marine heritage. Collections include china, glass, furniture, toys, tools, ship portraits and models, musical instruments and costumes, as well as a stage coach and a lighthouse lens. Housed in the same building, a 100-year-old former church, is a research library and archives. Here the visitor can find historical information about Yarmouth, including records, documents, photographs and genealogical material on town families. The Yarmouth County Historical Society cordially invites you to visit their museum and archives. Open year-round, hours vary by season.

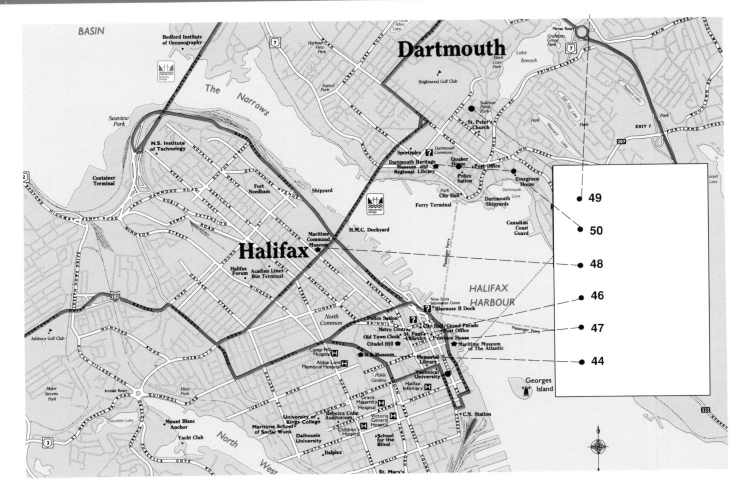

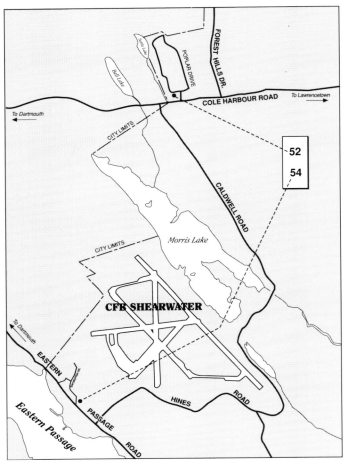

The Army Museum   p.46

P.O. Box 3666, Halifax South
Nova Scotia B3J 3K6
(902) 422-5979

The Army Museum is a non-profit institution located within the walls of the historic Halifax Citadel. Six renovated barrack casemates built in the 1820s house changing exhibits from the Museum's internationally recognized collection of small arms, uniforms and insignia. The Museum operates with assistance of The Nova Scotia Museum and Environment Canada, and in coordination with The Canadian War Museum. It is staffed daily. Visitors in December through April are requested to call since extensive exhibit refurbishing takes place during this period. Please note, assistance is available for visitors who have difficulty with stairs.

Cole Harbour Heritage Farm Museum   p.52

471 Poplar Drive
Cole Harbour, Nova Scotia B2W 4L2
(902) 434-0222

A project of the Cole Harbour Rural Heritage Society, this lively community museum is a rural oasis in a busy suburb. Perennial gardens, adjacent woods and a marsh rich in bird life add to this atmosphere. The Museum's buildings and artifacts, dating from the late 1700s to the mid 1900s, tell the story of local farming settlers who supplied Halifax with fresh food grown on the land and gathered in and around the area's rich saltmarsh. Farm animals and periodic farm activity demonstrations enliven the museum. Buildings include a modest saltbox style farmhouse, a mid-19th century barn of classic proportions and a 19th-century house. The Rose & Kettle Tearoom in the latter offers light refreshments; picnic tables are also available. Minutes from downtown Dartmouth, the Heritage Farm Museum is easily accessible by city buses. Please call for information on summer program of suppers, farmers' markets and other events. Open daily May 15-Oct 15, or by appointment at other times.

Dartmouth Heritage Museum and Historic Houses   p.50

Dartmouth, Nova Scotia
(902) 464-2300

Household furnishings and accessories, decorative arts, costumes and textiles, paintings, photographs and industrial artifacts depict the life and development of this community from first settlement in 1750 to the present day. The museum at 100 Wyse Road also houses a significant archival history of Dartmouth. Located at 26 Newcastle Street, **Evergreen Historic House** is a splendid example of 19th-century architecture. It was also the home of folklorist Dr. Helen Creighton for more than half a century. Equipped as an historic house of the mid- to late-Victorian period with objects drawn from the Museum's permanent collection, Evergreen also displays some 18th and 19th-century furnishings. **The Quaker Whaler House** at 59 Ochterloney Street is the only remaining building dating from the late 18th century. Its architecture and furnishings reflect the daily lives of the merchant class when Dartmouth was an important whaling port. Evergreen House and the Quaker Whaler House are open July and August; Dartmouth Heritage Museum, year-round.

Maritime Command Museum   p.48

Admiralty House
Gottingen Street at Almon
CFB Halifax, Nova Scotia B3K 2X0
Tel (902) 427-8250

The Maritime Command Museum was established in 1974 to collect, preserve and display the artifacts and history of the Canadian Maritime military forces. The Museum also maintains a library and archives relevant to naval history and the Dockyard since 1759. The Museum is located in Admiralty House, a National Historical Site built in 1814 as the official residence of the Commander-in-Chief of the British North American Station. The exhibits deal mainly with the history of the Royal Canadian Navy since its inception in 1910, and the Royal Navy and its influence on Halifax since 1759. Visitors use the Museum's own gate, which opens into its private gardens. Open year-round, hours vary by season.

Maritime Museum of the Atlantic   p.47

1675 Lower Water Street
Halifax, Nova Scotia B3J 1S3
(902) 424-7490

Located on Halifax's revitalized waterfront, the Museum focuses on the region's maritime history, including the tragic Halifax Explosion. Its open exhibit and display centre featuring six theme galleries offers a stunning, panoramic view of Halifax Harbour. Browse and ask questions in the restored 19th-century ship chandlery. Examine ship figureheads and tools of the shipbuilding trade in the Days of Sail gallery. Visit the Age of Steam exhibit to see models tracing the rapid development of ship design in the 19th-century. The history of the Royal Canadian Navy is featured, so is Sable Island, with its legacy of shipwrecks and heroic lifesaving efforts. Displays include small boats from working dories to pleasure craft and right outside the museum building, the retired Canadian Hydrographic Survey vessel *Acadia*, a national historic site, is permanently moored. The wharves also offer visitors a first-hand view of harbour traffic from various small craft to naval and merchant ships. Part of the Nova Scotia Museum Complex. Open year-round. Hours vary by season.

National Historic Sites in Metropolitan Halifax   p.45
Canadian Parks Service
Historic Properties
Upper Water Street
Halifax, Nova Scotia B3J 1S9
(902) 426-3436

Our national parks and historic sites offer an opportunity to discover Canada's unique natural and cultural heritage. While in the metro area, watch history unfold at the Halifax Citadel, York Redoubt and the Prince of Wales Tower. Inside the Citadel, the sounds of the city are exchanged for the crack of rifle fire and skirl of the pipes, as uniformed soldiers drill on the parade. Talk to a soldier's wife or explore the barracks, casemates and exhibits. Take a stroll in Point Pleasant Park and visit the Prince of Wales Tower, commissioned by Queen Victoria's father, Prince Edward, in 1796. Just outside the city you'll find York Redoubt, standing guard over Halifax harbour for 200 years. It's the perfect spot for a seaside picnic or for watching ships sail by. To discover all this and more, watch for the Beaver Symbol on highway signs. It will lead you to vacation experiences of a lifetime.

Nova Scotia Museum   p.44
1747 Summer Street
Halifax, Nova Scotia B3H 3A6
(902) 424-7353; fax (902) 424-0560

The Nova Scotia Museum in Halifax is far more than just the administrative heart of the provincial museum system. Visitors can take the measure of a huge whale, see displays of Nova Scotia's mammals in their natural habitats or view other examples of natural history, including an exciting new geology gallery. There are also special exhibits, collections of Nova Scotia furniture and displays of Micmac artifacts including an extensive collection of quillwork. Short-term in-house exhibits and travelling exhibits from local, national and international sources change approximately four times per year. Curators care for extensive provincial collections in natural history, archaeology, ethnology and domestic history and provide related exhibits, school and public programs. The Museum offers many public activities, and also has a research library and a curatorial reference centre. Open year-round. Hours vary by season.

Shearwater Aviation Museum   p.54
CFB Shearwater
Nova Scotia B0J 3A0
(902) 466-1083

Since 1979 the Shearwater Aviation Museum, an accredited Canadian Forces Museum at Canadian Forces Base Shearwater, has been dedicated to collecting, preserving, interpreting and exhibiting artifacts and information pertaining to Maritime military aviation. It traces this history in northeastern Canada from its beginnings in 1918 with United States Naval Air Service convoy escort operations at Baker's Point, Dartmouth, through the formation of the Royal Canadian Air Force in 1924, up to the present day. Exhibits highlight roles played in anti-submarine warfare, search and rescue etc. The Museum collection contains uniforms, photographs, documents and equipment, as well as aircraft. Six aircraft are on static display as Gate Guardians on the Base. Operational aircraft include a CP-121 Tracker and a Fairey Swordfish; others await restoration. Located in Warrior Block. Ask for directions from Base Main Gate. Hours vary by season.

Shubenacadie Canal Commission   p.49
Fairbanks Interpretive Centre
54 Locks Road
Dartmouth, Nova Scotia B2X 2W7
(902) 462-1826

The story of the Shubenacadie Canal is one of engineering triumph, business failure, human endeavour and hard work. Built in two periods, 1826-1831 and 1856-1861, the canal linked the commercial centre of Halifax with the trade route of the Bay of Fundy. From 1861 to 1870, steamboats and barges navigated the locks and inclined planes built to connect the lakes and rivers that formed the system. The development of the Intercolonial Railway, however, eclipsed the canal as an effective means of transportation. The Shubenacadie Canal Commission now operates two visitor centres and interprets a number of sites along the canal route. The trails around the canal cut and locks at Port Wallace are accessible year-round. Much of the canal route is navigable by canoe and the Canal Commission's long-term goal is to restore as much as possible to navigability for shallow-draft vessels. The visitor centres on Alderney Drive and at Port Wallace in Dartmouth are open to the public June 1 to Labour Day or by appointment.

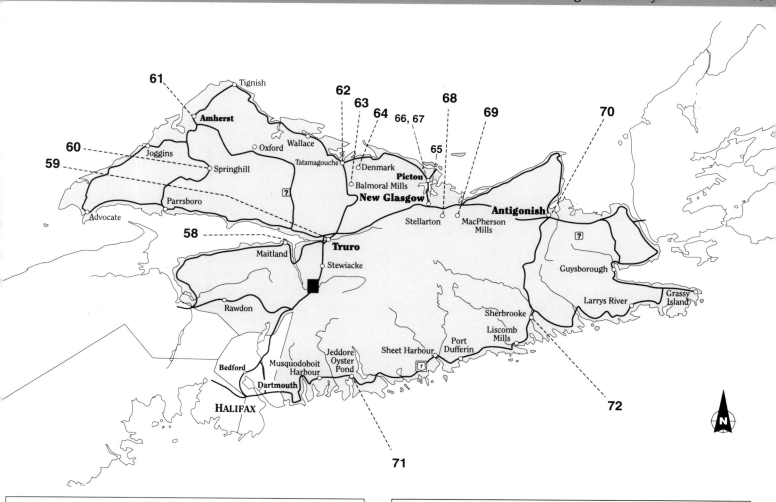

Antigonish Heritage Museum p.70

20 East Main Street
Antigonish, Nova Scotia B2G 2E9
(902) 863-6160

This general local history museum is located in the former railway station. Built in the early 1900s, it retains many of the original architectural features of that period and is one of the few remaining buildings of this style. Exhibits are rotated seasonally and in keeping with current events and special celebrations. Collections include pioneer artifacts, photographs, railway memorabilia and special exhibits. During the annual Antigonish Highland Games Week celebrations each July, tartans, clan and Scottish history are on display. Genealogical research resources such as local histories, census records, family histories and military information are housed in one of the railway waiting rooms. An inventory of local Heritage Homes and public buildings is also available. Operated by the Heritage Association of Antigonish with assistance from the Town and County of Antigonish. Open year-round except Christmas and New Year's Day, hours vary by season. Wheelchair accessible.

Balmoral Grist Mill p.63

Between Routes 311 & 326
Balmoral Mills, Nova Scotia
(902) 657-3016

Balmoral Grist Mill stands on a gorge in Matheson's Brook, between Earltown and Tatamagouche. Built around 1874 by Alexander MacKay, it was just one of five mills on the brook grinding wheat, oats, barley, rye and buckwheat into critically important supplies of flour, oatmeal and livestock feed during the 1880s. Although the mill was thought to have been powered by an overshot waterwheel, recent research shows that, in fact, the original power was a Leffel turbine. This power source will be added to the mill at a later date. Visitors can explore all three levels of the mill, see flour being ground and examine the mill's unique Scottish oat-drying kiln. Flour and meal are available for sale. A scenic park across the river offers a beautiful picnic setting with a magnificent view of the gorge. A part of the Nova Scotia Museum Complex. Open June 1 - October 15.

Colchester Historical Museum   p.59
29 Young Street, P.O. Box 412
Truro, Nova Scotia B2N 5C5
(902) 895-6284

A warm welcome awaits visitors to the Colchester Historical Museum located in the former Science Building of the provincial Normal School in downtown Truro. A fine example of late Victorian architecture, this building was constructed in 1901 of brick masonry with a red sandstone foundation. A wide range of permanent and temporary displays of agriculture, forestry, shipbuilding, railroading and pioneer life allow visitors to experience the human and natural history of Colchester County from its beginnings to the present day. The variety of exhibits cater to any interest and age. For visitors with a desire to delve more deeply into Colchester County heritage, a well-stocked and equipped research centre containing early township and cemetery records; birth, death and marriage records on microfilm; and extensive family genealogy records is available to the public. Township maps, local genealogy and history publications are on sale at the museum's Book Nook. Open year-round, hours vary by season.

Cumberland County Museum   p.61
150 Church Street
Amherst, Nova Scotia B4H 3C3
(902) 667-2561

Located in Grove Cottage, historical home of Senator R.B. Dickey, exhibits in this year-round museum provide a unique opportunity to explore Cumberland County's industrial, natural, artistic and social history. Library and archival facilities focus on industrial, labour and genealogical information. A designated heritage property and municipal art gallery, the museum provides solace during a busy travel schedule. Nature enthusiasts can stroll the grounds, admire the gardens, bird-watch or simply contemplate under giant elms and maples. Annual summer events include a Grove Cottage Luncheon in June and an Antique Mechanical Fair on the second Saturday in August. Open year-round, hours vary by season.

Fisherman's Life Museum   p.71
Route 7
Jeddore Oyster Pond, Nova Scotia
(902) 424-6478

The Fisherman's Life Museum illustrates the way of life of the inshore fisherman and his family at the turn of the century on the eastern shore of Nova Scotia. The family raised most of its food on the land, buying only commodities such as tea and sugar. The sale of fish and winter work in the woods provided the sole sources of cash. Built in 1857 by James Myers and remodelled several times, the modest house was later home to his youngest son's family of 13. It has been refurnished with the ordinary things of rural living from Nova Scotia fishing communities - a parlour pump organ, hooked mats, grandmother's favourite dishes and a woodstove - based on recollections of the family and community. The museum still brings back fond memories for many Nova Scotians. It is operated by the Nova Scotia Museum Complex. Open June 1 - October 15.

Hector National Exhibition Centre   p.67
Old Haliburton Road
P.O. Box 1210
Pictou, Nova Scotia B0K 1H0
(902) 485-4563

The *Hector* with her cargo of Scottish settlers was the first immigrant ship to land in Nova Scotia. Located in the historic shiretown, Pictou, the Hector Centre was established in 1973 to commemorate the bicentennial of the landing. Usually once a year the Centre displays its exhibit of this story. Tartans hanging from the ceiling create a colourful setting for artifacts and fascinating tales surrounding the story. Nearby, a replica of the *Hector* is under construction. As one of Canada's 23 National Exhibition Centres, the Hector Centre also features temporary and travelling exhibits of local, national and international scope. The Hector Centre Trust Archives specialize in Pictou County research material, including family and community histories; church, cemetery and shipping records, vital statistics, family genealogies, census records and local newspapers on microfilm with card index files. Open year-round, hours vary by season.

Lawrence House p.58
Route 215
Maitland, Nova Scotia
(902) 424-6478

When Lawrence House was built, around 1870, Maitland was one of Nova Scotia's prosperous ship-building communities. Owned by shipbuilder William D. Lawrence and his family, it is typical of the grand homes occupied by shipbuilders, owners and captains of the day. The house overlooks the Shubenacadie River and the upper reaches of Cobequid Bay where William Lawrence's shipbuilding yard was situated. Here he could work on ship plans and watch his vessels being built. In 1874 more than 4,000 people came to Maitland to witness the launching of the *William D. Lawrence,* the largest full-rigged ship ever built in Canada. The house has two large, formal Victorian parlours and many other rooms filled with original furnishings of the day. In 1965 Lawrence House was designated a National Historic Site. It is a branch of the Nova Scotia Museum Complex. Open June 1 - October 15.

The MacPherson's Mills Grist Mill p.69
Route 347
Pictou County, Nova Scotia
(902) 752-6266

Built by William MacPherson in 1861, MacPherson's Mills Grist Mill ground out oatmeal, wheat and buckwheat on its three sets of millstones for more than a century. Driven by water from the overshot wheel, the mill ran day and night when the season and the water were right. It was later converted to an 1880-model water turbine, which is still the source of power today. Across the yard is MacPherson's Mills Farm Homestead. It was built 130 years ago and in the winter of 1972, completely dismantled, repaired and reassembled at its present site as a typical farm homestead of the period. Parts of the house and its furnishings have been contributed by many people of the area so it can truly be considered an East Pictou farm home. Knowledgeable local guides will be pleased to show you the mill, the kiln, the farmhouse and the beauty of the river. Grist mill products and local handcrafts for sale. Open July and August.

McCulloch House p.66
Old Haliburton Road, off Route 106
Pictou, Nova Scotia
(902) 485-4563

McCulloch House was built around 1806 for the Reverend Thomas McCulloch, founder of Pictou Academy, first president of Dalhousie College and remembered as the father of liberal education in Nova Scotia. Constructed of bricks from Scotland, many exterior and interior features of the house remain unchanged, including one room furnished as Thomas McCulloch's parlour/study with several pieces of his furniture on display. In addition to being a minister and noted pedagogue, McCulloch pursued wide-ranging interests including natural sciences. The famous J.J. Audubon visited in 1833 to study McCulloch's work and pronounced his the finest private collection in North America. Look for a signed print titled *Labrador Falcon,* given by the great American naturalist to his friend. The Hector Centre Trust administers McCulloch House for the Nova Scotia Museum Complex. Open June 1-October 15.

Nova Scotia Museum of Industry p.68
Stellarton, Nova Scotia
(902) 755-5425

The Nova Scotia Museum has collected hundreds of artifacts from all over the province for a Museum of Industry scheduled to open in 1994. Incorporated into interpretive exhibits will be equipment large and small, tools, personal items and photographs representing Nova Scotia's industrial past. There are industrial locomotives, including *Samson,* built in 1838, the oldest surviving in Canada and the 17th oldest in the world. A 20-foot-high saw from the Wallace Quarries stands eye-to-eye with a huge Bucyrus-Erie steam shovel made at Maritime Steel, and a Caterpillar tractor used for road-building in the 1930s. Other large items include tea-bagging machinery, printing equipment, steam turbines, distillery equipment and several types of steel-making gear. Items, such as a Clairtone Hi-Fi, dating from the 1950s will bring back memories to many Nova Scotians. The photograph collection includes women working in munitions during both world wars and children in the workforce during an earlier era.

Sherbrooke Village   p.72
Box 295
Sherbrooke, Nova Scotia B0J 3C0
(902) 522-2400

Walk into Sherbrooke Village and step back in time. Restored beginning in 1969, this historic village is the older part of the town of Sherbrooke, recreated as it was more than a century ago. Twenty-five buildings constructed between 1860 and 1870 have been restored to reflect the period. Explore the church, schoolhouse, post office, blacksmith shop, jail and several homes. Furnished to the period, the houses reflect the lives of the wealthy and the humble. Above Cumminger Brothers' general store, visitors can don 19th-century costumes and be photographed using the contemporary ambrotype process. The boatbuilding shop still constructs wooden boats. The hotel serves 1880s-style fare, the telephone exchange still functions and the court house is still in use today. Nearby an operational water-powered, up-and-down sawmill and reconstructed lumber camp of the 19th century illustrate one of the original village's main activities. Operated by the Sherbrooke Village Commission for the Nova Scotia Museum Complex. Open June 1-October 15.

Springhill Miners Museum/ Anne Murray Centre   p.60
P.O. Box 610
Springhill, Nova Scotia B0M 1X0
(902) 597-8614

Visit the **Springhill Miners Museum** and tour a mine with experienced miners now working as guides. Descend safely with the guide and his lamp to explore the underground slopes of the Syndicate Mine. Swing a pick at the coalface many feet beneath the surface and take home a lump of Springhill coal as a souvenir. Museum exhibits include fossils, tools, gear, models, photos, displays and documents recording the town's often-tragic, century-long story of mining. It was also Springhill's destiny to be the home of a musical sensation known in entertainment capitals around the world as Anne Murray. Now, the **Anne Murray Centre** pays fitting tribute to the world-class achievements of this singing superstar. In a series of award-winning, three-dimensional and audio-visual displays you can see, first-hand, the awards, memorabilia and highlights of her exciting life and career. The specialty gift shop features unique souvenirs, tapes, CDs and prized Nova Scotia crafts. Both locations open seasonally, check locally for hours.

Pictou County Historical Museum   p.65
86 Temperance St.
New Glasgow, Nova Scotia
(902) 752-5583

Located on a tree-lined street in the heart of New Glasgow, the historic Stewart House preserves Pictou County's heritage and its ties with the past. Bequeathed to the town by descendents of the Carmichael family, shipbuilders and town settlers in the early 1800s, this stately home dating from the late 19th century is still set up as a home, with several rooms of original and contemporary furnishings. Other rooms house exhibits, such as a collection of glass from the Humphreys Glass Factory in Trenton, a flourishing enterprise during the the area's industrial heyday around the turn of the century when the County had a world-wide reputation for its shipbuilding and coal mining. Other exhibits include an extensive assortment of late-19th-century clothing, including underwear, and a large collection of farming implements and tools. The museum also houses the Pictou County I.O.D.E. and Boy Scout archives. Open daily June-September.

Sunrise Trail Museum   p.62
Main Street
Tatamagouche, Nova Scotia
(902) 657-9011

The old steam boiler and winch on the lawn of the Sunrise Trail Museum arouse curiosity about long-forgotten area industries. Visitors to the museum will see smaller tools and artifacts used in lumbering, shipbuilding, farming and fishing. The museum provides a panoramic story of our history beginning with the Micmac's first settlement along the shore, then on to the heartbreaking story of the Acadians whose expulsion from the North Shore first began here in Tatamagouche. The first permanent settlers, the French Protestants from Montbillard, France, were brought by the colourful Colonel DesBarres. Scottish settler Welwood Waugh came in 1778 and with his family began our first school, church and mill. Interesting pioneer life artifacts and memorabilia about the first professional people and community events complete the glimpse into our history. Guides are also available to answer questions. A loan display circulates new exhibits. Open daily July and Aug; weekends only in spring and fall. Inquire locally for hours.

Sutherland Steam Mill   p.64
Route 326
Denmark, Nova Scotia
(902) 657-3016 or 657-3352

When Alexander Sutherland built his sawmill in Denmark, Nova Scotia, in 1894, steam was replacing water as the most efficient way to cut logs. Alexander and his brother John Thomas established Sutherland Bros. & Co. with Alexander specializing in the manufacture of carriages, sleighs and sheds while Thomas looked after house construction. Carriages and sleighs were constructed, assembled and painted in the upper part of the mill. Doors and windows were also manufactured upstairs. The downstairs was used for general woodwork and custom work. The mill turned out much-needed lumber for England during World War II and its legacy is also still visible in the fancy gingerbread trim on many local houses. The mill's restored steam boilers, including a Robb-Armstrong (No.835) 6x6 inch engine manufactured in 1904 but patented in 1897, and machinery are operated several times during the season. Part of the Nova Scotia Museum Complex. Open June 1 - October 15.

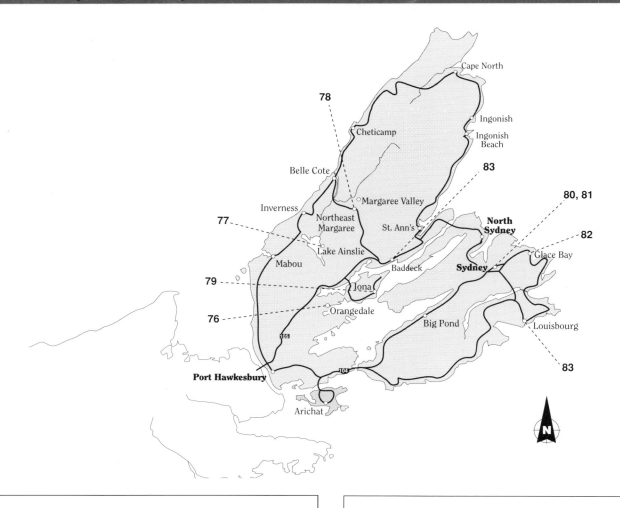

Cape Breton Miners' Museum   p.82
42 Birkley Street, Quarry Point
Glace Bay, Nova Scotia B1A 5T8
(902) 849-4522; fax (902) 849-8022

Located on a 15-acre, oceanside site, the Miners' Museum offers a unique blend of history and heritage. It was erected as a testimonial to the coal mining industry of Cape Breton as well as the miners who labour deep in the earth and far out under the Atlantic Ocean. A highlight of any visit to the Museum is an underground tour of the Ocean Deeps Colliery, an actual slope mine located within the building. Retired miners guide the tours, offering detailed information on mining methods as well as sharing their own first-hand experiences. The Miners' Village on the same site features a Company Store or 'Pluck Me' and a duplex Company Home depicting conditions around 1850 and at the turn of the century. A third wood-frame building has been transformed into a beautiful 65-seat, licensed restaurant featuring the hospitality and service for which Cape Breton is famous. Open year-round, hours vary by season.

Cossit House   p.80
75 Charlotte Street
Sydney, Nova Scotia
(902) 539-1572

Believed to be the oldest house in Sydney, Cossit House was built in 1787 by the Reverend Ranna Cossit, the first Protestant minister assigned to permanent duty in Cape Breton. It was home to him and his family until 1800 when Bishop Inglis, hoping to calm a turbulent local situation, transferred the politically controversial Reverend Cossit to Yarmouth. The simple one-and-half-storey house had many owners and several alterations over the years until it was acquired by the Nova Scotia Government in 1975 and restored as closely as could be determined to its 18th-century appearance. Several rooms have been furnished based on an 1815 inventory of Reverend Cossit's estate. The house is operated by the Old Sydney Society as part of the Nova Scotia Museum Complex. Guides in period costume conduct tours and provide fascinating information about Cossit's colourful life. Open June 1-October 15.

MacDonald House Museum p.77
Route 395
East Lake Ainslie, Nova Scotia B0E 3M0
(902) 258-3317

Located on a hillside overlooking beautiful Lake Ainslie, the MacDonald House site consists of four buildings and more than two acres of land. Built about 150 years ago, the house is a good example of early Gothic design. Displayed inside is an interesting variety of furniture and artifacts, including two pre-1830 pioneer chairs and an antique loom. The barn, built in 1928, is now used for displays and activities throughout the summer months, including a barn dance on the second Saturday of July each year, during the summer heritage festival. A display shed houses an excellent selection of farm machinery and implements. A one-room schoolhouse, relocated to the site and furnished with a collection of two-seater desks, old textbooks and manuals, provides a pleasant trip down memory lane for many visitors. The Lake Ainslie Historical Society invites you to stop by to enjoy a relaxing tour surrounded by one of the most beautiful views in the province. Open seasonally.

Margaree Salmon Museum p.78
N.E. Margaree, Nova Scotia B0E 2H0
(902) 248-2848

A visit to this area is incomplete without a stop at the Margaree Salmon Museum. Located just 300 yards off the Cabot Trail at North East Margaree, it provides a rare look at the history of salmon fishing - and poaching - on the picturesque Margaree River. The museum appeals to far more than those who ply the rod. For the art enthusiast there are paintings and drawings; for those interested in history it is a gold mine. Readers will discover a fine collection of natural history books and for genealogists there are anecodes and photographs galore. Children are fascinated by the model of the river and the aquarium containing young salmon and trout. Since opening in 1965, the museum has accumulated a wealth of artifacts and information, and was expanded in 1978. Its work in preserving and interpreting the history of angling on the Margaree resulted in an award from The American Association for State and Local History - a much-coveted recognition. Open seasonally.

National Historic Sites on Cape Breton Island p.83
Canadian Parks Service
c/o Tourism Distribution Centre
P.O. Box 1448
Sydney, Nova Scotia B1P 6R7
800-565-9464

Our historic sites on Cape Breton Island offer an opportunity to discover Canada's unique cultural heritage. Visit Baddeck and learn about the life and work of Alexander Graham Bell. Let us introduce you to the invention of the telephone and Bell's pioneering achievements in flight, hydrofoils, genetics and medicine. Then, head to Glace Bay and the site where Guglielmo Marconi made telecommunications history with the first wireless message sent across the Atlantic. Travel to the Fortress of Louisbourg and step back in time to the summer of 1744. Stroll the busy streets and talk to the merchants, fishermen, soldiers and other townsfolk. Enroute to Cape Breton, visit Grassy Island and find out how the colonial cod fishery played an important role in the struggle for control of North America. Follow the Beaver Symbol on highway signs to explore our rich history of adventure and discovery.

Nova Scotia Highland Village p.79
P.O. Box 58
Iona, Nova Scotia B0A 1L0
(902) 725-2272; fax (902) 725-2227

The Nova Scotia Highland Village at Iona is a museum dedicated to those settlers who came to our province from the Highlands and Islands of Scotland. On a hillside overlooking the beautiful Bras d'Or Lakes, the museum consists of ten historic buildings ranging from a full-sized replica of a Hebridean Black House to an early 20th-century school house and store. Every summer costumed guides provide information to visitors as our buildings come to life with the sights and sounds of another time. Several special events are planned each summer including Highland Village Day (a full day of traditional music) held on the first Saturday in August, traditional cod fish suppers, workshops on Gaelic language and culture, and other musical presentations. Our Reception Building also houses *Highland Roots,* a computerized genealogy program designed to help visitors trace their Cape Breton ancestry. A small gift counter offers a good selection of Gaelic books and Celtic music. Exhibits open seasonally, reception building year-round.

Old Sydney Society   p.81
225 George St.
Sydney, Nova Scotia B1P 1J5
(902) 539-1572

Operated by the Old Sydney Society, a complex of museums set within old buildings invites visitors to explore Sydney's past. **St. Patrick's Museum,** built in 1828, is the oldest Roman Catholic church and cemetery on Cape Breton Island. Within its stone walls, local memorabilia trace the history of this Loyalist town. Walking tours of the city's historic North End daily. The **Jost House** was built in 1787. Restored, it shows the evolution of a family dwelling over two centuries. Climb from the basement's 18th-century kitchen to the main floor's early-Victorian parlour, to a collection of thematic displays on the third floor. Once the only variety theatre east of Montreal, the Lyceum constructed in 1904 now houses **Cape Breton Centre for Heritage and Science,** a venue for changing exhibits on natural and cultural heritage. Children's programs, films and lectures. All three locations have museum shops and are open year-round, hours vary by season.

The Orangedale Station   p.76
Orangedale, Nova Scotia
(902) 756-3384

The last remaining of 17 stations built for the InterColonial Railway of Canada, the Orangedale Station is the last still standing on its original site. As a museum it now collects for display, artifacts and railroad data on the historical and cultural aspects of the Short Line-Main Line through Cape Breton Island. This station, built of solid wood timbers, enjoyed much in common with its 'sisters' along the Line, architecturally, economically and socially. Restoration began in 1988. The spacious office, waiting rooms and station master's apartment offer an introduction to a lost romance of life linked to the railroad era. Visitors are invited graciously to 'take tea' in the upstairs dining room and assorted rail theme items and crafts are available in the Last Whistle Stop shop. Accessible from exit 4 of TransCanada Highway 105, or by water; a government wharf on the Bras d'Or Lakes is just a stroll away. Open seasonally, the Station welcomes all.

MUSEUMS INDEX

Museums book photo credits

With the exception of the following pages, all photographs in this book were taken by Ron Merrick and Roger Lloyd, courtesy of Education Media Services of the Nova Scotia Department of Education.

Anne Murray Centre: 60 Top

Antigonish Heritage Museum: 70

Blair House: 36

Canadian Parks Service: 31, 45

Kerry DeLory: 46

Department of National Defence: 54

Rosemary Eaton: 52-53

M.F. Gaul Photography: 61

Warren Gordon: 82

Knickles Studio: 20-21

Shirley Locke: Back cover, 69

Maritime Command: 48

Pictou County Historical Museum: 65

Shirley Robb: 60 Top

Settlers' Museum and Cultural Centre: 22

Sunrise Trail Museum: 62

Alex Wilson 30

Edith Wolter: 18-19,